Tell It Slant

poems by

Marcy Llamas Senese

Finishing Line Press
Georgetown, Kentucky

Tell It Slant

Copyright © 2020 by Marcy Llamas Senese
ISBN 978-1-64662-319-8 First Edition
All rights reserved under International and Pan-American Copyright Conventions. No part of this book may be reproduced in any manner whatsoever without written permission from the publisher, except in the case of brief quotations embodied in critical articles and reviews.

ACKNOWLEDGMENTS

"Song of Summer Days" and "Pipecleaner Man" appeared in the *San Diego Poetry Annual*, 2015-16. Garden Oak Press: Rainbow, California.

"Trees" appeared in *Summation* 2017/18, *Ekphrastc Anthology*. Longboard-to-Tipperary Press: Escondido, California.

Publisher: Leah Maines
Editor: Christen Kincaid
Cover Art: Diane Stacey, "Echoes from the Jungle;" www.dianestacey.com
Author Photo: TJ Devadatta Best, www.LightInspiredArt.com
Cover Design: Elizabeth Maines McCleavy

Order online: www.finishinglinepress.com
also available on amazon.com

Author inquiries and mail orders:
Finishing Line Press
P. O. Box 1626
Georgetown, Kentucky 40324
U. S. A.

Table of Contents

Song of Summer Days 1

The Cape 2

Dream Corridors 3

Pipecleaner Man 4

Vigil 6

Gage's Woods 9

Trees 10

Blanket of the Night 11

The Dancer and the Dream 12

Visitation 13

Love's Embrace 14

I Don't Know 16

Waiting 17

Tell all the Truth, but tell it slant—
Success in Circuit lies.
Too bright for our infirm delight,
The truth as lightning to the children eased
With explanation kind.
The truth must dazzle gradually—
Or every man be blind.

Emily Dickinson

Song of Summer Days
(for Paul)

While the air is still thick with heat
the children play fiercely,
beating the deep drum,
the endless song of summer days.

Faces turning darker or redder
from the receding heat,
they come to the field
where trees are dark and grass turns cool—
all, all slowly fades
into the embers of twilight.

Morning comes again, so soon
after the short summer night.
Bicycle wheels flash
as the children ride through the dew
like cartwheels in the rain,
humming the song of summer days.

There is no past,
only the sunlit hour of their play,
only the shouts of their own unyielding joy
inflaming asphalt and air,
echoing the song of summer days.

Memory, with its
relentless wearing down,
leaves only a glimpse of that tireless play,
a pale shadow of summer days,
as the light slowly fades
into the embers of twilight.

The Cape
(Madrid)

The matador walks slowly across the ring,
head bent at that perfect angle.
Surging roars, cape against sky,
sound against skin—
all soft edges in my memory.

Gentle whispers, a cool white arm—
my mother lifts her stole
as a curtain before my eyes,
musky odor of thick fur fills my nostrils.

The moment I didn't know
we were waiting for unfolds
beyond the edges of my mother's shawl—
the bull breathes his last breath.

I remember the red cape and bright sun,
my mother's white arms,
the matador a hero.

Dream Corridors

In the dream,
I woke to her voice
calling, calling me
to come in.
I hurried through the dark hallway
to her closed door,
crying out to her
as she had done for me
as a child, after a bad dream.

I stood in the stillness, waiting.
She finally opened the door
but didn't speak.
She stood staring over my shoulder
at something I couldn't see.

"Don't worry," I said,
"I'm here now."
The words tasted like dust
against the roof of my mouth.

Suddenly, she stooped quickly and licked
my hand, a small rough tongue
against my palm, her eyes bright
against the darkness of the hall.

Pipecleaner Man

1.

"Popeye," we'd call him.
Sitting on my father's lap,
inhaling the perfume of his pipesmoke,
my brother and I take turns
squeezing his bulging biceps.
Their hardness seems permanent,
like the warmth of summer days.

I remember holding hands
with my father,
my dress a stiff cloud,
white patent leather shoes
bright with newness.

I slip on the curb—
Dad's hand tightens around my wrist,
traffic rushes by our feet.
I am caught,
dangling by the thread
of his strength.

2.

Last night I watched him struggle
up the stairs, dragging his suitcase
behind him. He said goodnight,
wrapped his thin arms around my neck.
I hug him back, and remember
the pipeleaner men he'd make for me
as a child—stiff limbs bent sharply
at knee and elbow.

Feeling the jutting planes
of his shoulder blades
pressing against my hands,
wondering at the melting of muscle and sinew
into slopes and peaks,
I hold him closer.

Vigil

I
The moonlight slants blue
across my father's face,
his eyebrows knit close,
willing his breath to flow.
I sit on the edge of a straight-backed chair,
wanting to caress his hand,
afraid to disturb his fitful sleep.

> *Some nights Dad screamed at us,*
> *fists pounding against the arms of his recliner.*
> *Other times he wouldn't speak at all,*
> *his crossword puzzle on his knee,*
> *pipe smoke around him*
> *an impenetrable fog.*

"In or out? Do I breathe
in our out?" He asks the same question
several times during the night,
and I say, "Well, Dad,
first breath in,
then out.
Just in,
then out.
In...
out..."
I try to match
his uneven cadence,
my words like a chant that lull him back
into the nightmare of half-sleeping
and not breathing.
He will wake again to ask,
and I will chant,
and he will sleep
to wake again.

*I crouched beside my father
in front of the hole he dug,
a mound of rich dirt inside waiting to be crowned
by a tangle of rose root and branches.
He reached both hands into the hole,
scooping up the black soil in his large palms,
letting it crumble between his fingers,
saying, "See? Isn't it beautiful?"*

I never sleep.
Looking at the world outside the window
bathed in blue light,
I wonder at the stillness
that doesn't enter the room
where I keep my vigil.

My father cries out—
"Oh, my God."
I lean over him,
try to see where it hurts.

He rises, pushes me away,
strides down the hall in front of me,
determined to hunt sleep down.
He is barefoot, pajama bottoms
hanging loose around his bony hips.

I trot to keep up,
dragging his blanket and pillow
behind me.

He took off his belt,
that slender curve of black leather.
I dared him to touch me
and he swatted my arm.
That was it—I walked out,
didn't come home that night.
We didn't speak for weeks,
despite my mother's pleas.

II

The waiting
seems like a dream now,
the dream of blue moonlight
against unshaven cheekbones.
I lie in my bedroom,
a small white dresser gleaming in the corner
like a white stone you find on a walk
and put in your pocket,
rubbing your finger
against its round coolness.

Gage's Woods

I walk to Gage's again,
find a pine tree to lie under.

Through the jagged needles
I glimpse moonlight and stars.
The pungent scent of woods and summer nights
stings my nostrils,
the hum of night frogs ebbs and flows.

I listen harder, try to uncover
what's underneath,
what drew me to lie cradled here
in this fragrant pine bed.

I stay longer than usual,
hoping to startle the secret out of hiding.
Walking slowly home—
that warm circle of yellow light—
I miss the trees.

Later I dream of pine woods.

Trees

Lashing myself
to a rough trunk torso
with my skinny child-arms and legs,
as high as I can scramble
in shorts and tennis shoes,
the wind bends the living, leafy being
that I try to embrace with my whole body.
The tree is dancing in the wind,
and I am moving with it,
longing to be launched into flight,
like the birds beyond my reach.

Later, in adolescent angst,
waking to some inner call
that draws me into the clear winter night,
I walk alone among the trees,
see tracings of darker branches
against a midnight blue sky,
seeking answers in the silent etched darkness.

Now, in this later autumn of life,
I know to seek solace among the trees,
to lean against their smooth or rough bodies,
find shelter under their silent arms,
listen to the wordless melodies
of leaves and needles.

The language of their slow wisdom
seeps into my skin
like water into thirsty spring soil.

Blanket of the Night

Blanket of the night,
I want to pull down your splintered rays
onto my waiting skin,
let your radiance feed my hungry heart.

I want to lie on the desert floor—
sand pressing into every crevice of my spine—
and feel the tender weight
of your sparkling vastness.

Only you
can quiet the restless humming
of my mind.

Only you
can warm me
with your cool light.

The Dancer and the Dream

The dancer is me.
Or it is many dancers,
and they are not me.

I long to make a dance
that snaps underfoot like running hard on ice,
or hangs suspended in the air,
like jasmine on a summer night—
a dance that looks like wind sounds,
lifting and sighing through the trees.

The dance is like horses running wild
under a full moon.
They are not meant to be caught,
only dreamed.

Visitation

The dream begins:
silence.
An empty train platform
stretches in front of me,
my back to the station.
Beyond the end of the platform,
 the curve of the tracks
melts against the horizon.

Suddenly,
impossibly,
 my mother is there—
walking towards me
from the far end of the platform.

I hear the click of her heels,
see her tiny feet
in her favorite black velvet pumps.
She is radiant,
unquenchable,
her beige cashmere swing-coat
billowing around her.

I stop wondering how she came to be here,
how I came to be here.
I run to her.

She gathers me against her breasts,
whispers against my hair,
"I'm fine now, sweetie."
And I believe her perfume,
the warmth of her body against mine.

Love's Embrace

1.

Holding him in the bowl of my being—
cradled against my breast—
my fingers brush his bare head
and I am touching you again.

2.

We are alone, like lovers.
You sleep, and I watch you.
Your breath comes in ragged heaves,
lips caked with white threads
of cracked skin. Even in your sleep
you pull at the oxygen tubes
pressing against your nostrils.
Your wide, untrimmed nails
spread like wings
at the tips of your fingers.

I reach to touch your bare head,
wanting to feel skin against skin,
your life against my hand.
You hated that—
the indignity of baldness.
I thought it was beautiful
on you.

But now, your skin brittle like rice paper,
I smooth lotion across the bareness
that you never wanted me to mention,
much less touch,
and I whisper to you,
my child, my friend,
and try to soothe away your fear.

3.

Holding him
my breath leaves me in a single leap,
his cries distant.
My tears soak his shoulder
remembering you.

I Don't Know

"I don't know anything,"
you often said.
That was your wisdom.

I don't know
how to live without you.
My life feels unfamiliar
without your voice in it,
without your hands on either side of my face.
I don't know
when I will stop missing you.
Probably never.

The sound of the riding lawnmower
is someone else, not you—
you never took the easy way out.
You reached into the woodstove barehanded—
no gloves, no fear of the flames
laced around your fingers like star trails.

The wound will heal over,
not tear open again
when someone says your name,
just tremble beneath the surface—
the rumbling of memory.

Waiting

Grief
is like a tsunami,
tearing the heart from its roots
as it sweeps through the chest
and pools in dark puddles on the floor.

Nothing is left in its wake
but the soft mud of memory,
sliding through my fingers.

But now, so soon after,
love comes
like a slow flood of grace,
seeping into the heart
through the crevices,
through the cracks and fissures
left by grief's roaring tide.

I stand in the warm water,
its caress a soft murmur at my feet,
and await your embrace.

Marcy Llamas Senese is a poet who also expresses her creative energy through dance and music. Her poems have appeared in the *San Diego Poetry Annual* and *Summations*, a journal of art and poetry. She received her PhD in English from Indiana University of Pennsylvania, and studied creative writing at Hollins College while completing her Master's in Liberal Studies. Her career teaching writing and directing writing centers at the college level has allowed her to be mentored by her colleagues as well as her students. Currently, she is participating in modern dance performances through community-based and authentic movement projects in the San Diego area. She is also expanding her background in classical piano to include jazz improvisation and devotional music. She lives in the Golden Hill neighborhood of San Diego.

www.ingramcontent.com/pod-product-compliance
Lightning Source LLC
LaVergne TN
LVHW041525070426
835507LV00013B/1836